From: Your fond friends

Rita & Stan Oakley

God Bless & every Happiness

in your new surroundings

6th December '80

Royal Family Library

Prince Andrew & Prince Edward

CRESCENT – New York

Introduction

HRH Prince Andrew Albert Christian Edward was born at Buckingham Palace on 19th February 1960, the second son and third child of Queen Elizabeth II and the Duke of Edinburgh. He was the first child to be born to a reigning monarch for one hundred and three years, and the first to be named Andrew for five hundred years.

His younger brother, HRH Prince Edward Antony Richard Louis, the third son and fourth child of Queen Elizabeth II and the Duke of Edinburgh, was born at Buckingham Palace on 10th March 1964. The Queen's family was now complete with a gap of sixteen years between the birth of the oldest son, Prince Charles and the youngest son, Prince Edward.

The two young Princes led a secluded life at Buckingham Palace for a time. In fact, the first time Prince Edward appeared in public was in 1965 after the Trooping the Colour Ceremony when his mother held him up in her arms for the crowd to see.

Prince Andrew began school lessons at the age of four and, even earlier, was taught to ride by the Queen. Prince Edward also learnt to ride at an early age – when he was two. Being an expert horsewoman herself, the Queen was anxious that all her family should share her love of horses.

Both boys were christened in the Music Room, overlooking the gardens at Buckingham Palace. The ceremonies were conducted by the Archbishop of Canterbury, and only relatives and close friends were present. Each baby was dressed in the christening robe of Honiton lace designed for the baptism of Queen Victoria's children and also worn by Prince Charles and Princess Anne. The font was brought from Windsor specially for the occasion. However, the Queen was anxious that publicity photographs of these two christenings should not be taken and that the two younger children should be kept out of the public eye until it was absolutely necessary.

Prince Andrew became an enthusiastic member of the First Marylebone Cub Scout pack and attended meetings at Buckingham Palace. He was such a keen scout that when he went to his first boarding school, Heatherdown (where Angus Ogilvy had been a pupil), a special pack was formed so that he could continue to follow his interest.

Prince Andrew's education at Heatherdown was a break with the tradition established by his father and Prince Charles of attending Cheam School in Surrey. Later he followed their example and went to Gordonstoun, too.

To his great joy, in 1967, he was given a scaled down 'James Bond' version of an Aston Martin car which he had great fun with. He learned to drive under the tuition of the late Graham Hill and as soon as he passed his driving test (first time!) was able to drive himself whenever possible.

Gordonstoun was a very different school from the one the Duke of Edinburgh and Prince Charles had attended. When Prince Andrew was sent to Scotland in 1973, he found that, in common with many other Public Schools, it was partly co-educational, admitting girls as pupils. The Prince was able to enjoy a much more relaxed atmosphere and, unlike Prince Charles, enjoyed school, and did well there academically.

During his time at Gordonstoun, Prince Charles spent six months in Australia, at Timbertop. Prince Andrew had a similar break from school in Britain, spending six months at Lakefield College, Toronto in Ontario. His meeting with the Canadians was an immense success.

After a short time at a London day school, Prince Edward, followed Prince Andrew to Heatherdown and has now gone to Gordonstoun in the steps of his brothers and his father.

Prince Andrew began his public duties in 1976 when he accompanied his parents to the Olympic Games in Montreal. There he was able to cheer on his sister who was competing in the Equestrian Events as part of the British team. Prince Edward went with his family but played a much less prominent role in events than his elder brother.

Gradually, Prince Andrew began to take on more and more royal duties and was a very popular figure at many functions during the Queen's Silver Jubilee in 1977.

In September 1979, Prince Andrew followed the example of his elder brother, his father, grandfather and great-grandfather and joined the Royal Naval College at Dartmouth as a Midshipman to begin his career in the Royal Navy. His future is, as yet, undecided, but he is sure to do whatever he decides on with his characteristic vigour and enthusiasm.

Prince Edward is still a schoolboy with no plans for his future revealed, but his upbringing and sensitivity will surely enhance whatever role he decides to play in life.

Early Days

Prince Andrew was a lively youngster with an impish nature which endeared him to many but annoyed a few. He loved practical jokes and clowning, so one of the highlights of his young life was a birthday party at which the chief entertainer was the great Coco the Clown. As a child the Prince was known for such mischievous tricks as pouring bubble bath into the Royal swimming pool at Windsor, putting 'whoopee' cushions on chairs to frighten the unwary, charging the Royal corgi pack in his pedal car and tying the laces of the guardsmen outside the Palace! His father, Prince Philip often engaged him in gentle fights and, it is said, that after a well aimed blow from his son the Duke had to attend a public engagement sporting a black eye.

Prince Edward, on the other hand, is quiet and sensitive, and said to be the most artistic and contemplative of the Queen's children. However, he is very keen on outdoor pursuits as well, and began riding lessons at the early age of two, encouraged by his mother. At six he was awarded a prize by the Queen for riding in a Royal mews brougham which won the Concours d'Elegance trophy.

As photographs of their early life indicate, the two Princes had a happy babyhood, spent largely in the company of their family and relations. They were often pictured on Royal journeys to Sandringham or Balmoral.

All the Royal family has a genuine love of animals, particularly horses and dogs. The Queen was the first to introduce the breed of corgi dogs into the family when she was a child, and she still has many corgis as well as labradors and other breeds in her care. Her children have been lucky enough to learn at first-hand the characteristics of contrasting breeds of dog.

Left *An early picture of Prince Andrew in the arms of his mother, seen here leaving for holiday at Sandringham in December 1961, with Princess Anne by his side.*
Opposite *One of the early pictures of Prince Edward, with his mother on the 28th July 1964.*

Opposite *Prince Andrew and Prince Edward in the Music Room at Buckingham Palace. Prince Andrew smiles as he hugs his younger brother.*
Above *The blue-eyed, fair-haired Prince Edward in the arms of his nanny at King's Cross station on Sunday 15th August. He was leaving for Balmoral in the royal train. His first taste of Scotland!*
Left *A charming study of the Queen with Prince Edward and one of her corgis.*

Left *With a firm grip on the hand of his nanny, Prince Andrew sets off for a holiday at Balmoral. He looks a little over-awed at all the hustle and bustle.*
Below *At Windsor Castle, the Queen holds Prince Andrew in her arms. She spent as much time as possible with her son when he was young.*
Opposite *Prince Andrew climbing on to the back of a toy dog for a ride round the nursery.*

Above *A smiling Prince Andrew in the nursery with some of his toys – a brightly painted wooden train and a big friendly teddy bear.*
Above right *Prince Andrew trying to interest Prince Edward in a storybook.*
Right *Prince Andrew indulging in a game of peek-a-boo in the School Room at Buckingham Palace.*
Opposite above *An informal study of the Royal family at Windsor Castle. The Queen holds Prince Edward in her arms, while the rest of the family watch Prince Andrew's progress up the steps.*
Opposite below left *Prince Andrew waves enthusiastically from the window of a railway carriage as he and his mother and younger brother set off for a family holiday.*
Opposite below right *Prince Andrew sits astride the trunk of a tree in the Buckingham Palace gardens while Prince Edward waits below.*

Above left *Prince Andrew holding some toys as he poses for a photograph in informal surroundings at Buckingham Palace.*

Above *Prince Andrew and Prince Edward in the grounds of Buckingham Palace in February 1966 with two of their dogs, Whisky and Sugar. Prince Andrew is busy raking up the fallen leaves.*

Left *At Liverpool Street station in January 1966, Prince Andrew holds the lead of one corgi while a second jumps out of the railway carriage on to the platform.*

Opposite above *The two young Princes peep through the balustrade of the terrace at Buckingham Palace.*

Opposite below *Nearly five, Prince Edward shares a lesson with his cousins and friends in the School Room at Buckingham Palace.*

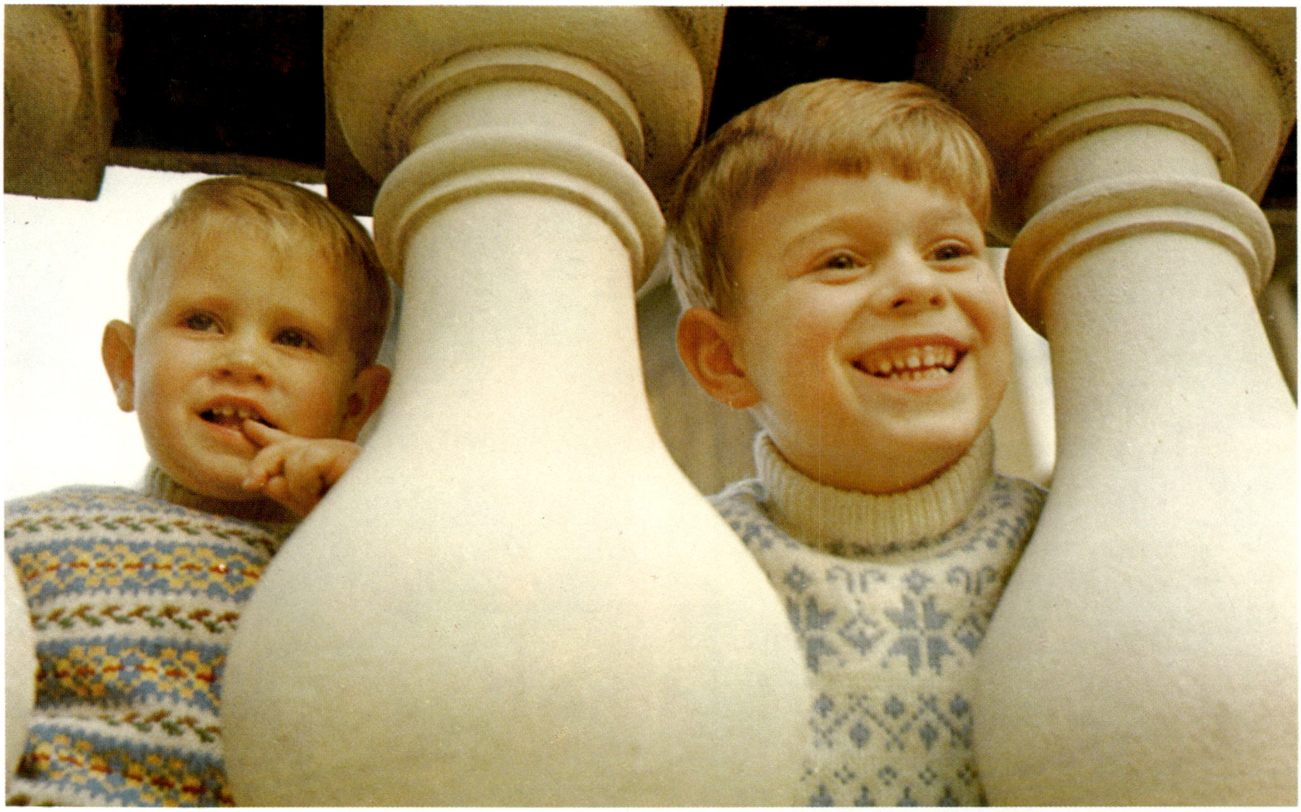

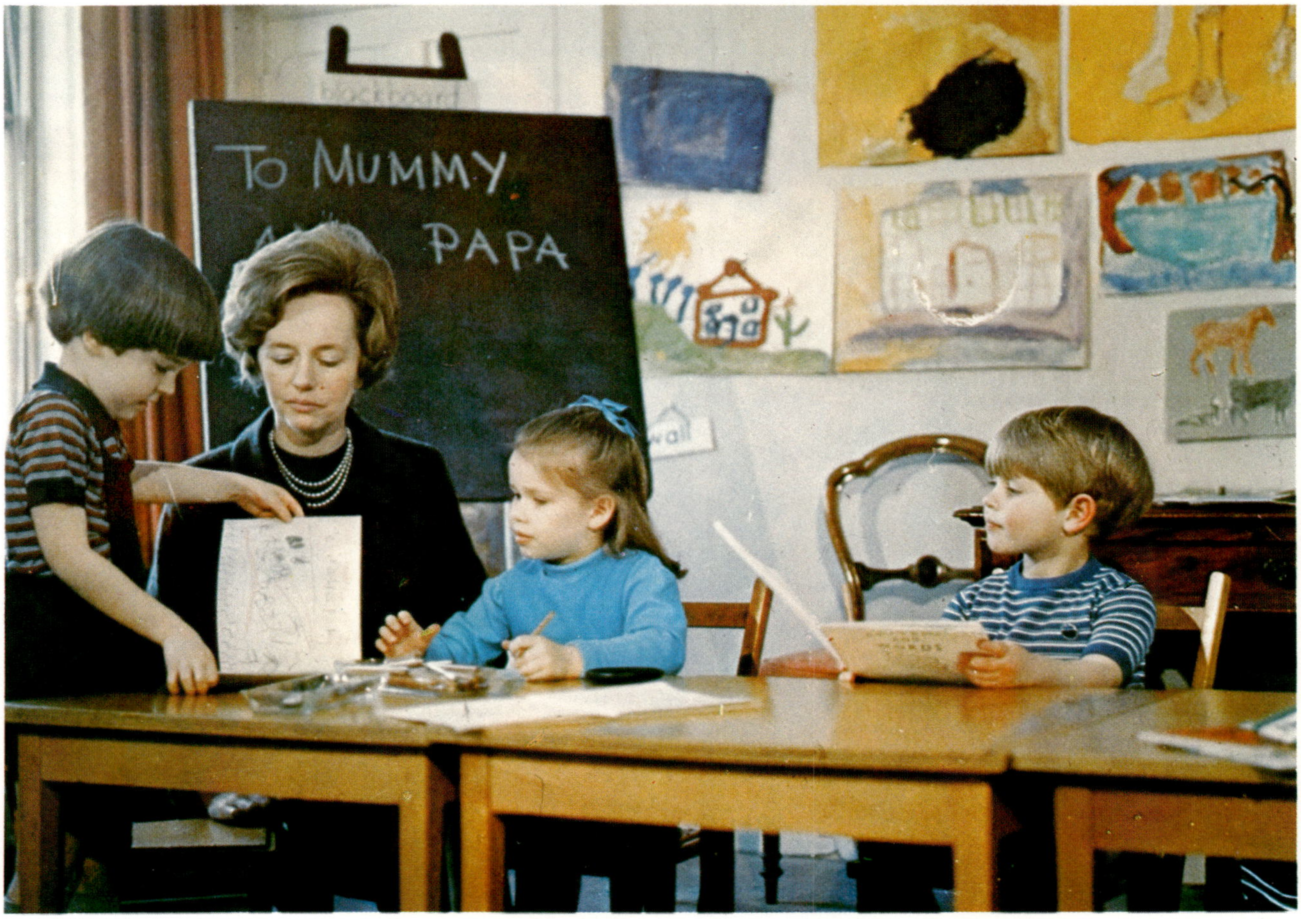
blackboard
To MUMMY
PAPA
wall

Above left *Taking an early interest in polo, Prince Andrew watches a match with a young friend. Some ponies can be seen in the background.*
Above *The Hill House School crocodile out for a walk in London, led by Prince Edward.*
Left *Pictured in July 1968, Prince Andrew proudly wears the uniform of the St Marylebone Cub Scouts (The Fighting First), of which he was an enthusiastic member.*
Opposite *A study of the young Prince Edward in a pensive mood.*

Above left *The Queen holds on to Prince Edward's hand as they walk in Windsor Great Park, accompanied by Prince Andrew.*
Above *With his cousins, Lady Sarah and Viscount Linley Armstrong-Jones, Prince Andrew attends the special premiere of the film, 'The Railway Children' in December 1970.*
Left *Field glasses at the ready, Prince Edward watches events at the Badminton Horse Trials which are enjoyed by all members of the Royal family.*
Opposite *A close up of Prince Andrew enjoying the scene at the Badminton Horse Trials.*

Life in Public

As befits Royal Princes, Prince Andrew and Prince Edward have had to learn the lesson of public appearances from an early age. They were performing their first Royal duties when most children would be enjoying games. One of Prince Andrew's early tasks was to present a bouquet to his mother at the Braemar Games in Scotland.

Prince Edward carried out one of his first public duties, in the full glare of the television cameras, when he acted as page at his sister's wedding in 1973. The Prince, in kilt, carried Princess Anne's train at her marriage to Captain Mark Phillips at Westminster Abbey. Lady Sarah Armstrong-Jones was the bridesmaid.

At school, Prince Andrew's life was kept as private as possible, and this included an exchange visit to a school in France. The Prince spent three weeks, with fifteen other pupils from Gordonstoun, in Toulouse to improve his French. He stayed with a French family, using an alias to preserve his anonymity. But he did make a public appearance at the Concorde factory nearby during his trip.

When he was sixteen, Prince Andrew spent two terms at Lakeside College, Toronto, Ontario in Canada and greatly endeared himself to the Canadians who even formed a fan club. Girls were seen wearing T-shirts with the words 'I am an Andrew Windsor girl' across them! During his stay, he played an intensive part in the sport and outdoor activities of the College. The highlight was a two hundred and eight mile canoe trip to the arctic northwest, sleeping under canvas. He returned to Gordonstoun for exams.

In 1976, Prince Andrew and Prince Edward accompanied their parents to the Olympic Games in Canada. The following year saw them play an increasing part in public life during their mother's Silver Jubilee.

Opposite *The Queen, accompanied by the late Lord Mountbatten, with Prince Andrew and his cousin, Viscount Linley, at the British Hovercraft Corporation at Cowes in August 1968.*
Below *Prince Andrew reaching up to pin a rosette on the bridle of a winning pony at the Royal Windsor Horse Show in May 1966.*

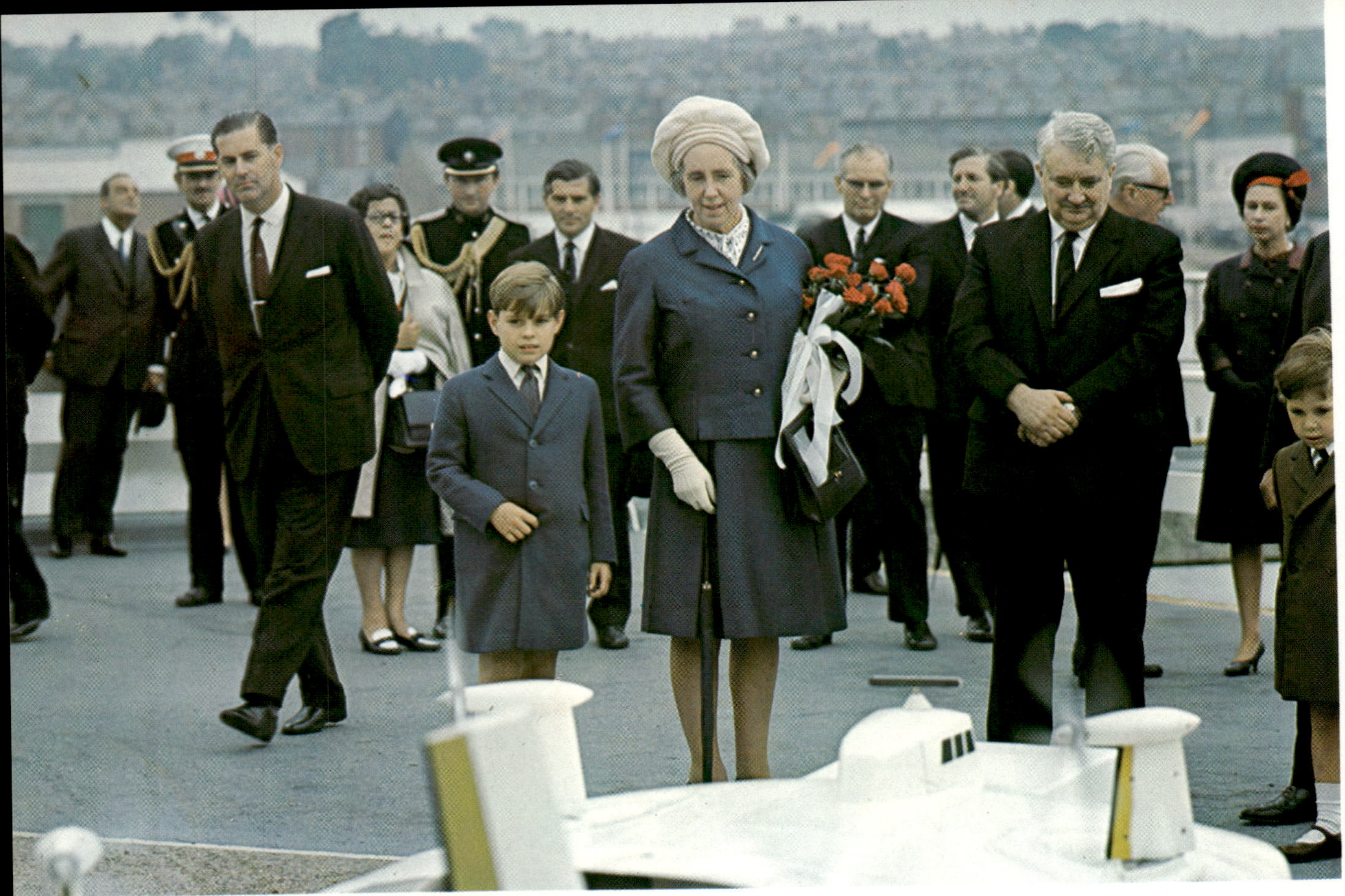

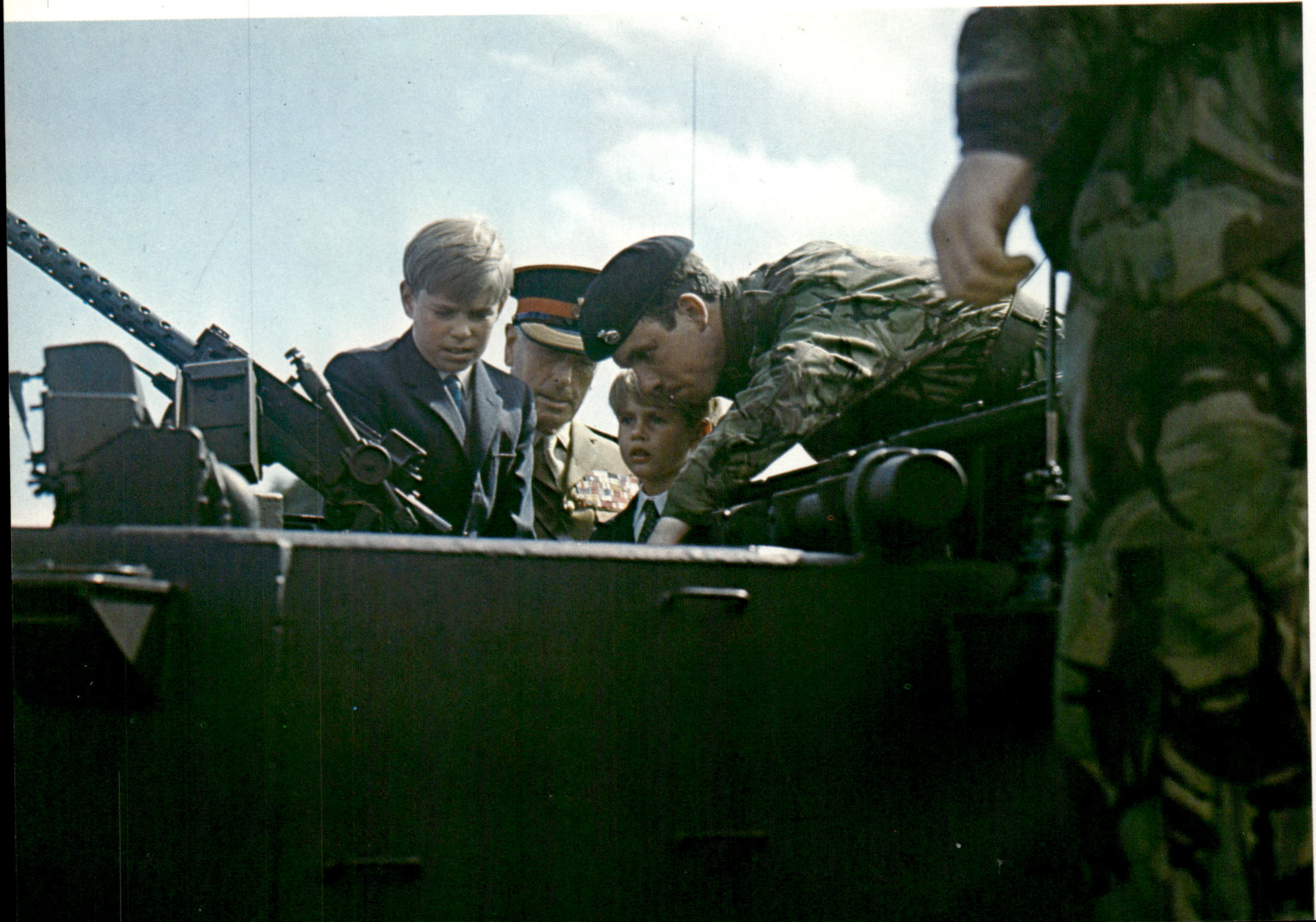

Opposite above *Prince Andrew shows a keen interest in one of the craft at the British Hovercraft Corporation at Cowes in August 1968. The Queen can be seen chatting in the background.*
Opposite below *Prince Andrew and Prince Edward on tour of the Army Exhibition at Aldershot in August 1971.*
Right *The Queen appearing at a public function with Prince Edward and, in the background, her sister Princess Margaret.*
Below *A formal welcome for a kilted Prince Edward, who with Prince Charles and his mother and father attended the annual Braemar Games in Scotland.*

Left Prince Edward leaving Buckingham Palace in an open carriage, watched by cheering crowds.
Below left After Trooping the Colour in June 1972, the Queen, in uniform, explains a point to Prince Edward. Her Majesty is seen wearing a black arm band in mourning for her uncle, the Duke of Windsor. At the ceremony a special lament was played in his memory.
Below right On a private visit to Oslo with his parents, Prince Edward is enthralled by the actions of the seals in the pool.
Opposite A view of the seals performing for the Royal party in Oslo.

Left *The Queen with her three sons at the Montreal Olympics in 1976.*
Above *Prince Charles and Prince Edward arriving in Canada for the 1976 Olympic Games.*

Below *Three royal princes informally dressed at Bromont during the 1976 Olympic Games in Canada.*

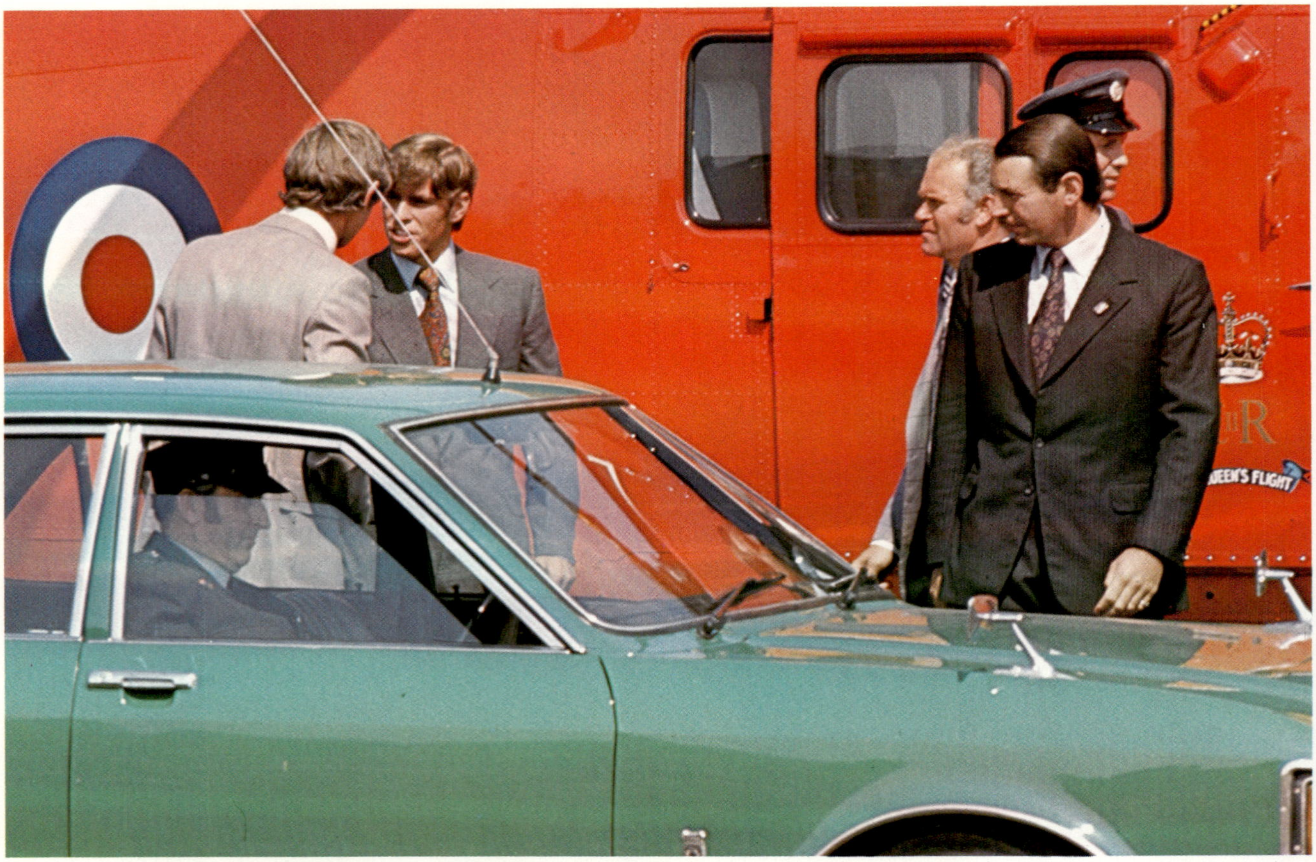
FLIGHT

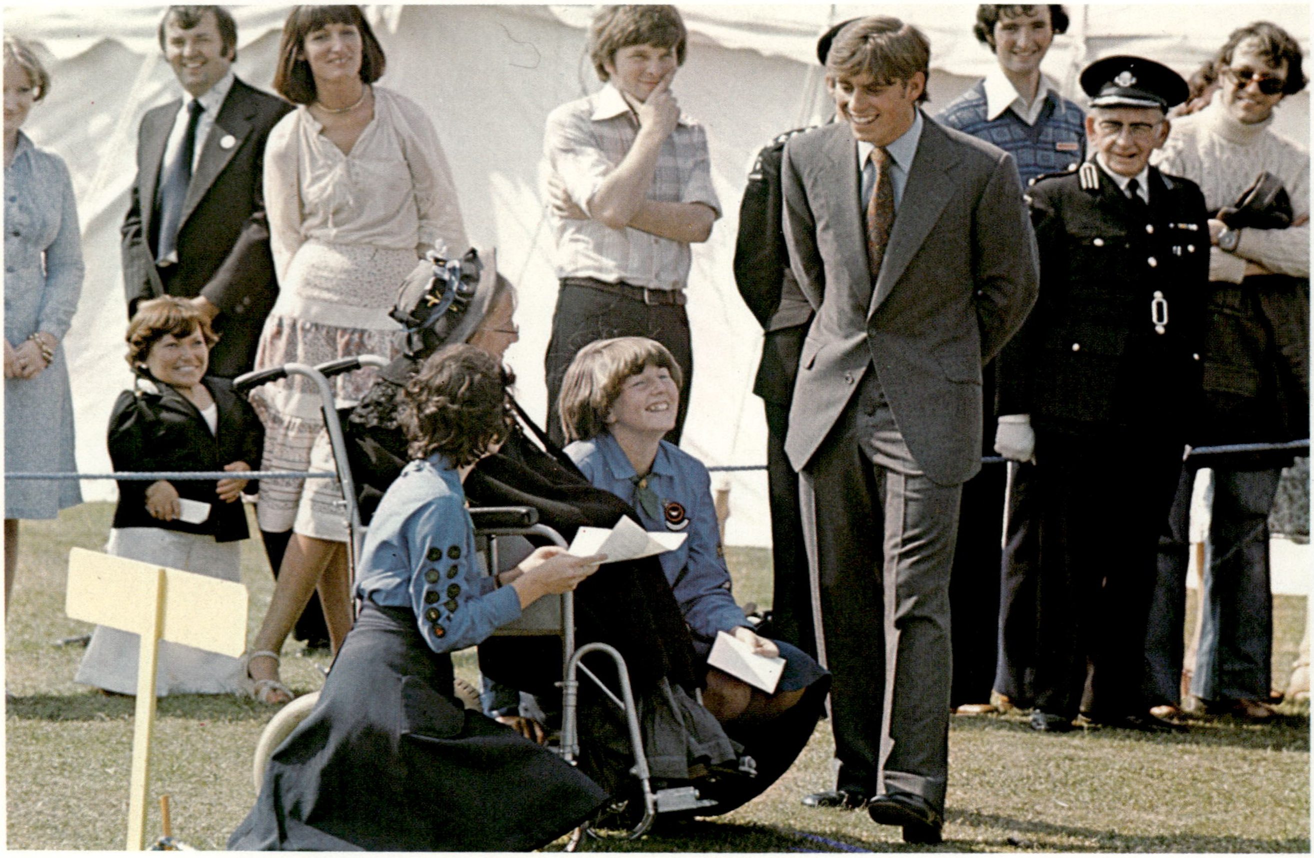

Opposite above *As part of the 1977 Silver Jubilee Celebrations, the Royal Family visited Northern Ireland. Prince Andrew arrives in Ulster via helicopter.*

Opposite below *Prince Andrew soon endeared himself to the people gathered to welcome him.*

Below *Here, Prince Andrew is seen talking to officials during his visit to the Province.*

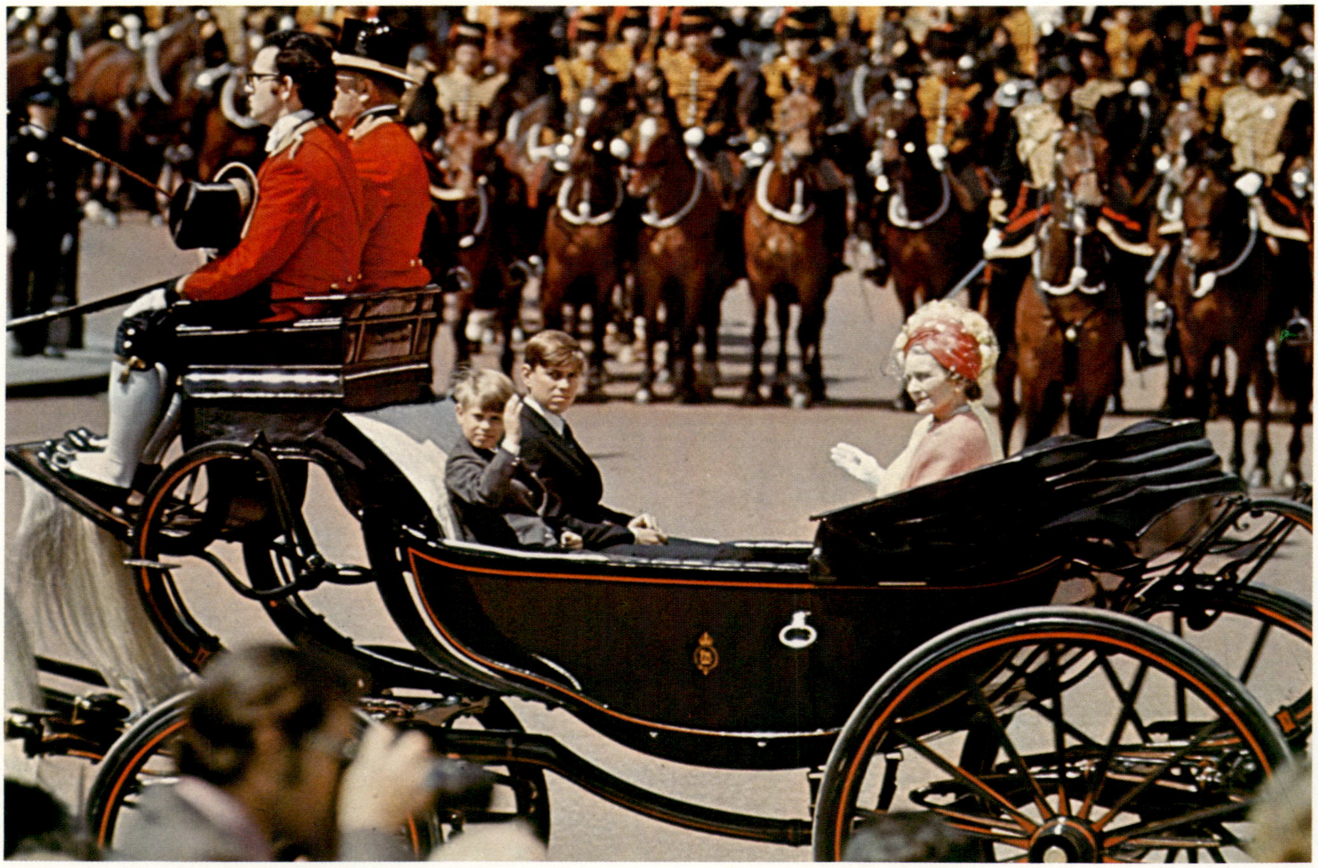

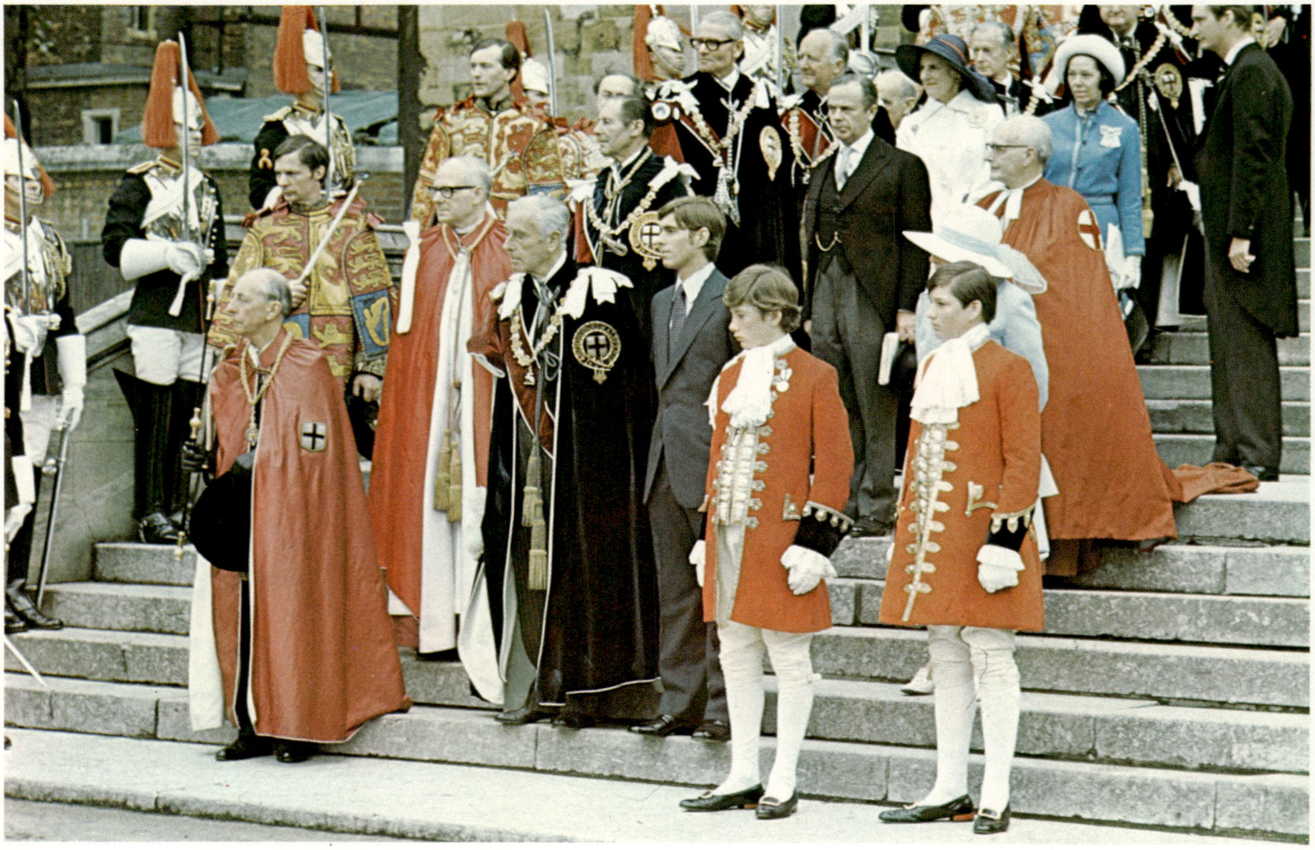

Opposite above *In Jubilee Year 1977, Princes Andrew and Edward on their way to the Jubilee Thanksgiving Service in St Paul's Cathedral, on 7th June*
Opposite below *Prince Andrew, taken on 13th June 1977, during Jubilee Year, watching the departure of his father and mother after the annual Ceremony of the Knights of the Most Noble Order of the Garter at St George's Chapel, Windsor. The late Lord Mountbatten, himself one of the Knights of the Order, is with him.*
Right and below *Prince Andrew and Prince Edward with their grandmother, the Queen Mother, during the Jubilee Thanksgiving Service in St Paul's Cathedral on 7th June 1977. Princess Margaret is sitting next to Prince Edward.*

Opposite *In 1977, while at Lakefield College School, Prince Andrew was a keen spectator at the Calgary Stampede Rodeo.*
Right *Prince Charles, who was touring Canada at the time, joined Prince Andrew to watch the annual Calgary Stampede.*
Below *The Princes wearing matching stetsons! Prince Charles and Prince Andrew in the traditional 'cowpoke' hats were eagerly watching the annual Calgary Rodeo. The finer points of the contest were explained to them by champion cowboys.*
Below right *A close up of Prince Andrew enjoying the spectacle of the Rodeo in Canada in 1977.*

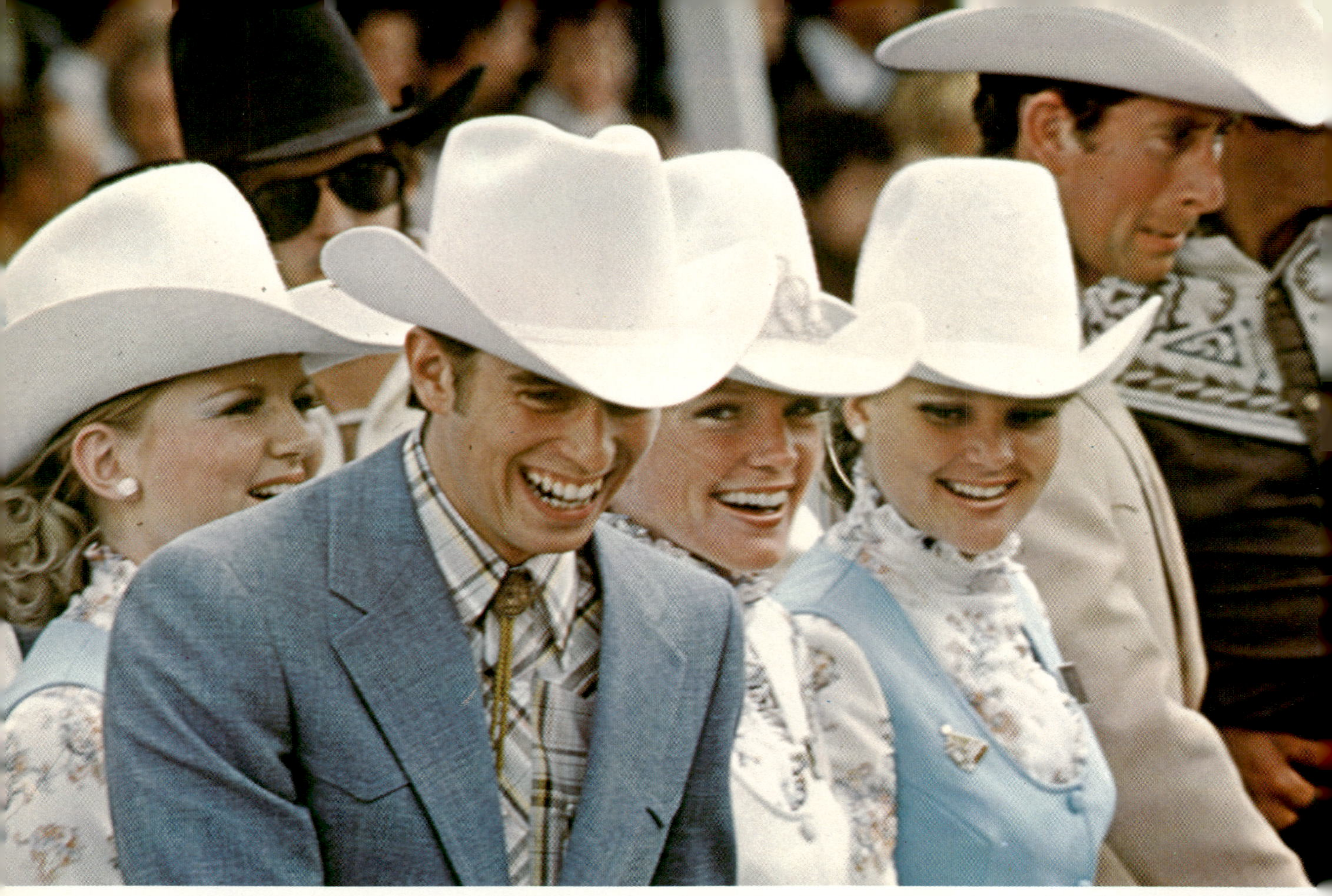

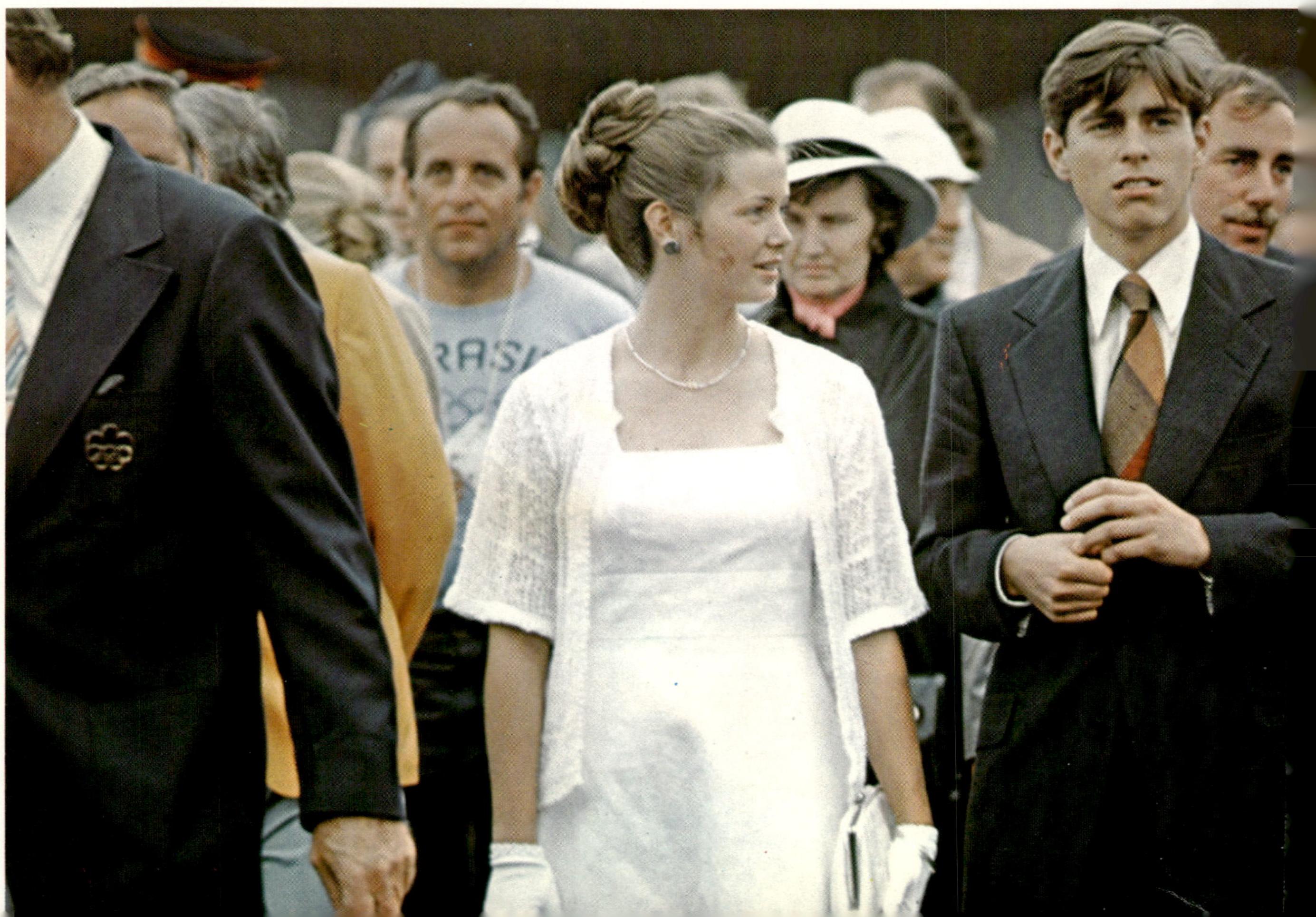

Opposite *Prince Andrew captivates a group of pretty girls at the Rodeo. All the party are wearing the traditional stetsons and are in high spirits.*
Below *Prince Andrew's appearance with Sandi Jones aroused a lot of public interest. They had first met at the 1976 Olympics in Montreal.*
Right *Prince Andrew looking smart in white safari suit, while on a trip to Tanzania with his mother.*

Above *Prince Andrew on the bridge of Prince Charles' command, HMS* Bronington. *As he was soon to follow his brother and join the Royal Navy, he was taking a keen interest.*
Left *In the company of his grandmother, Prince Edward tours HMS* Bronington *then commanded by his brother, Prince Charles.*
Opposite *Prince Andrew and Prince Charles accompany their grandmother, the Queen Mother, at the Braemar Games in Scotland.*

34

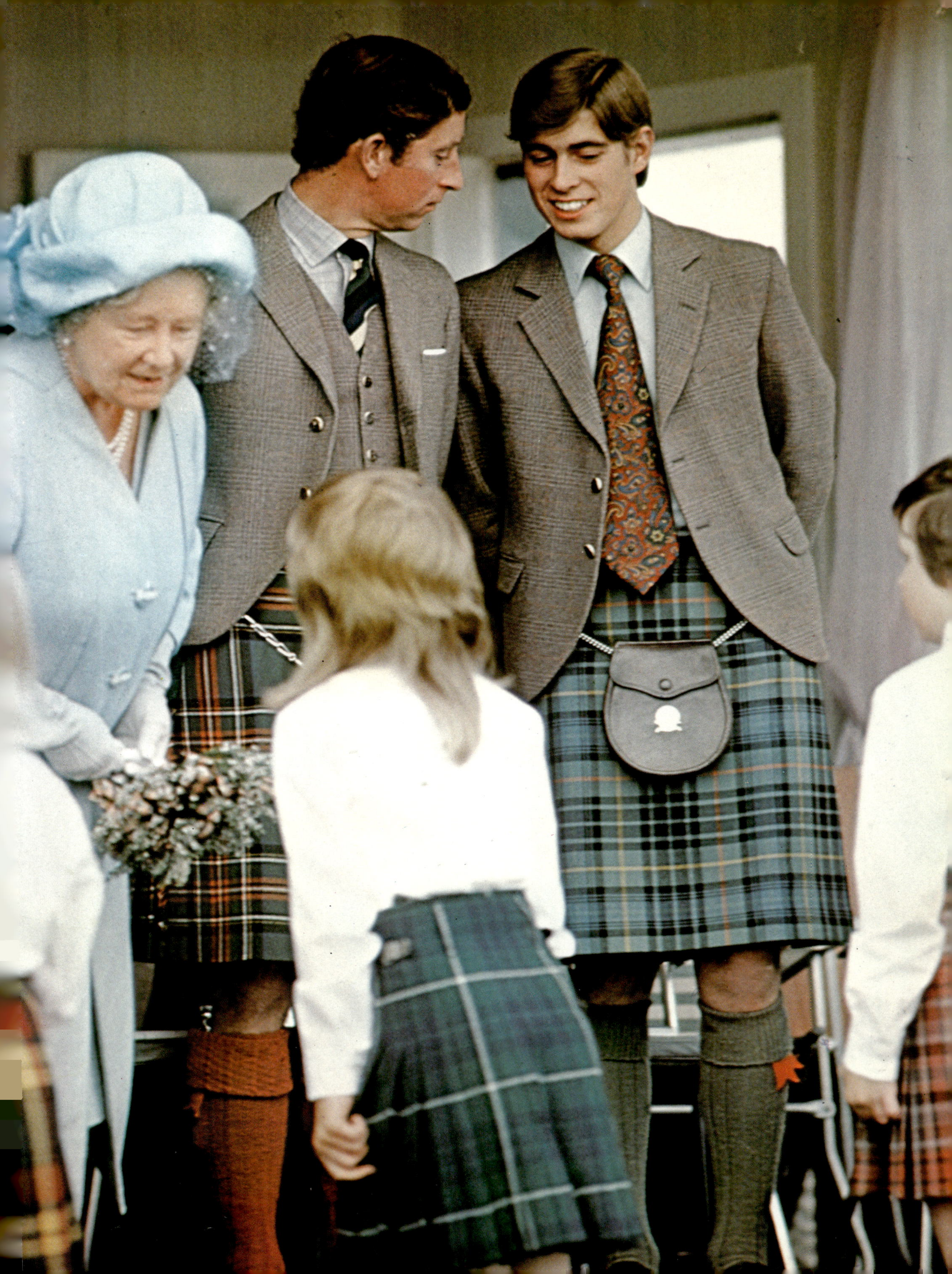

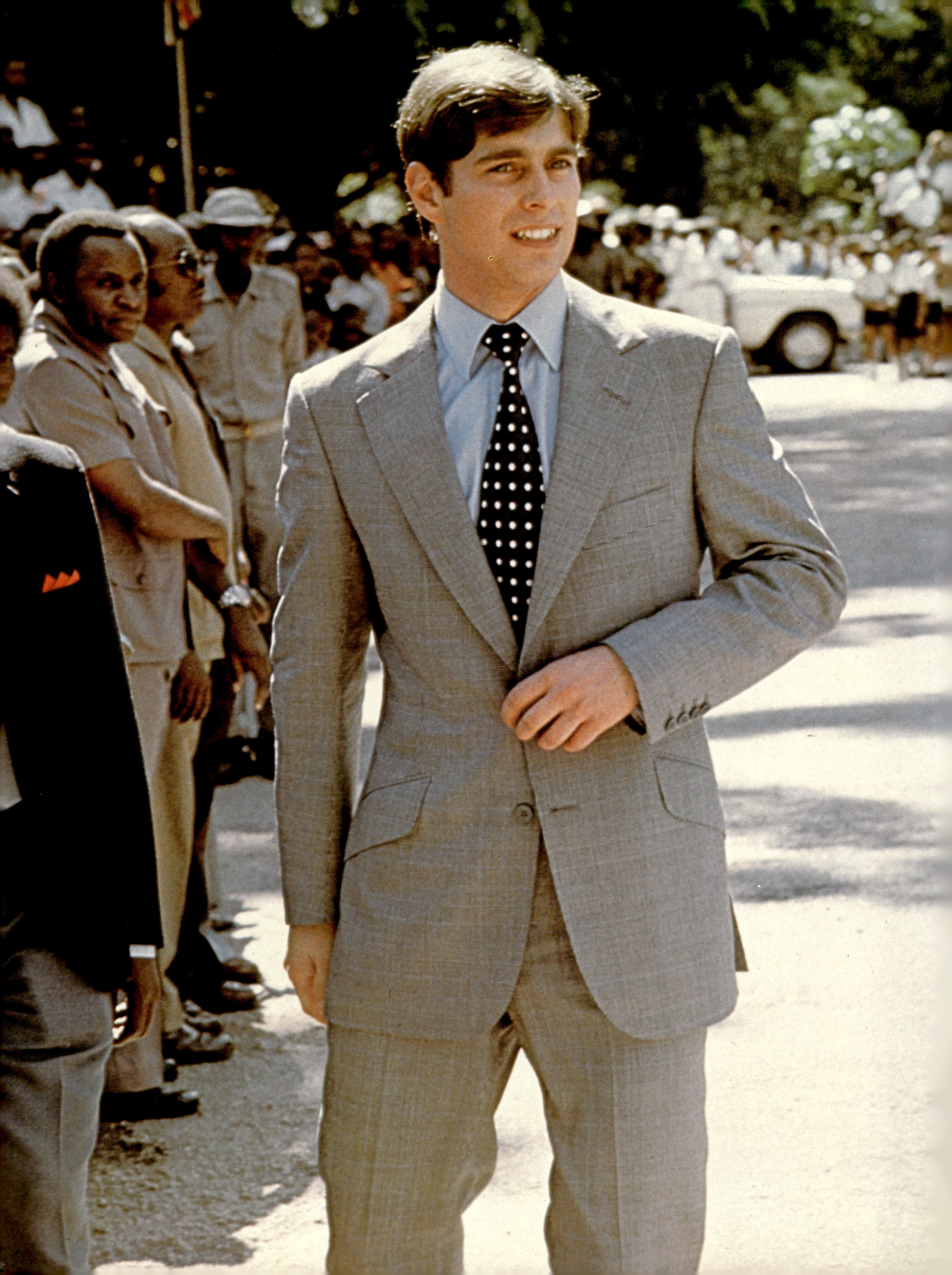

Opposite *Prince Andrew in Tanzania. He accompanied his mother the Queen on her recent trip there.*

Below *Prince Edward at the Olympic Games in Canada in 1976.*

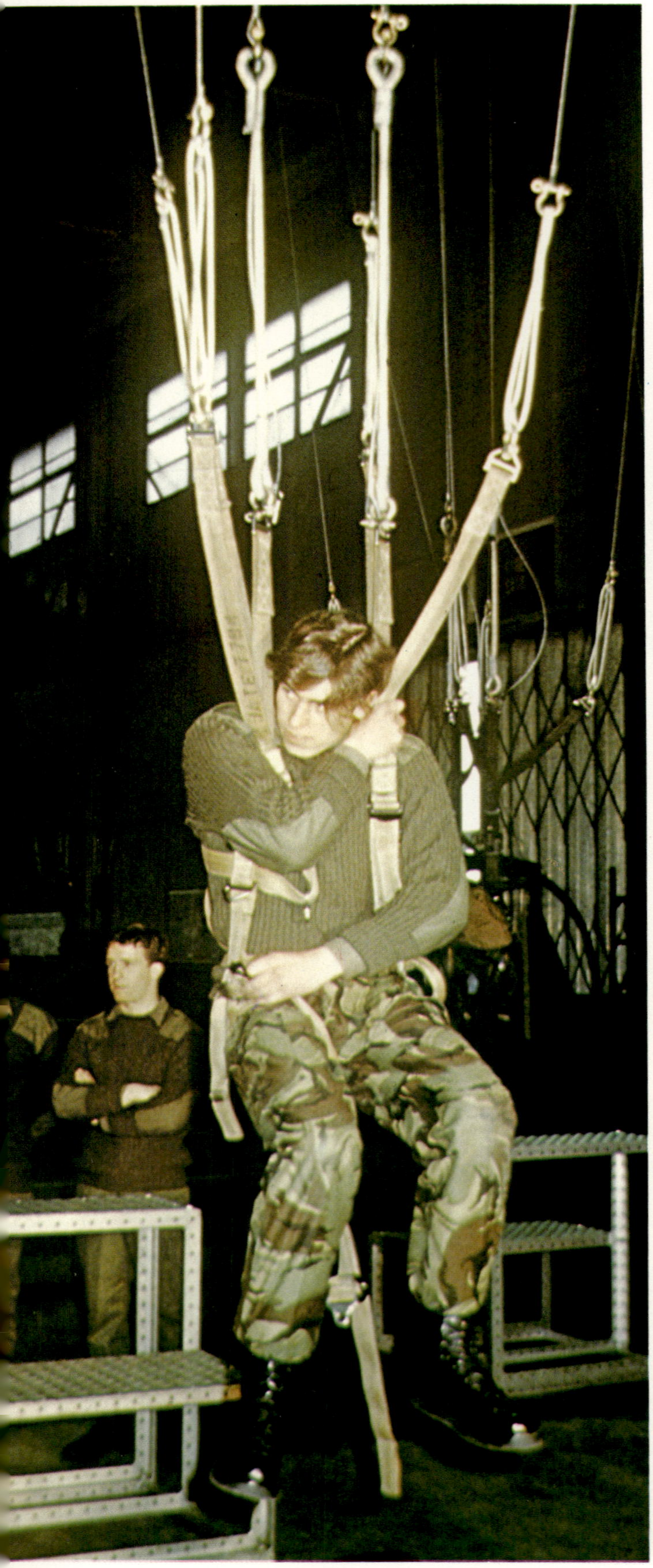

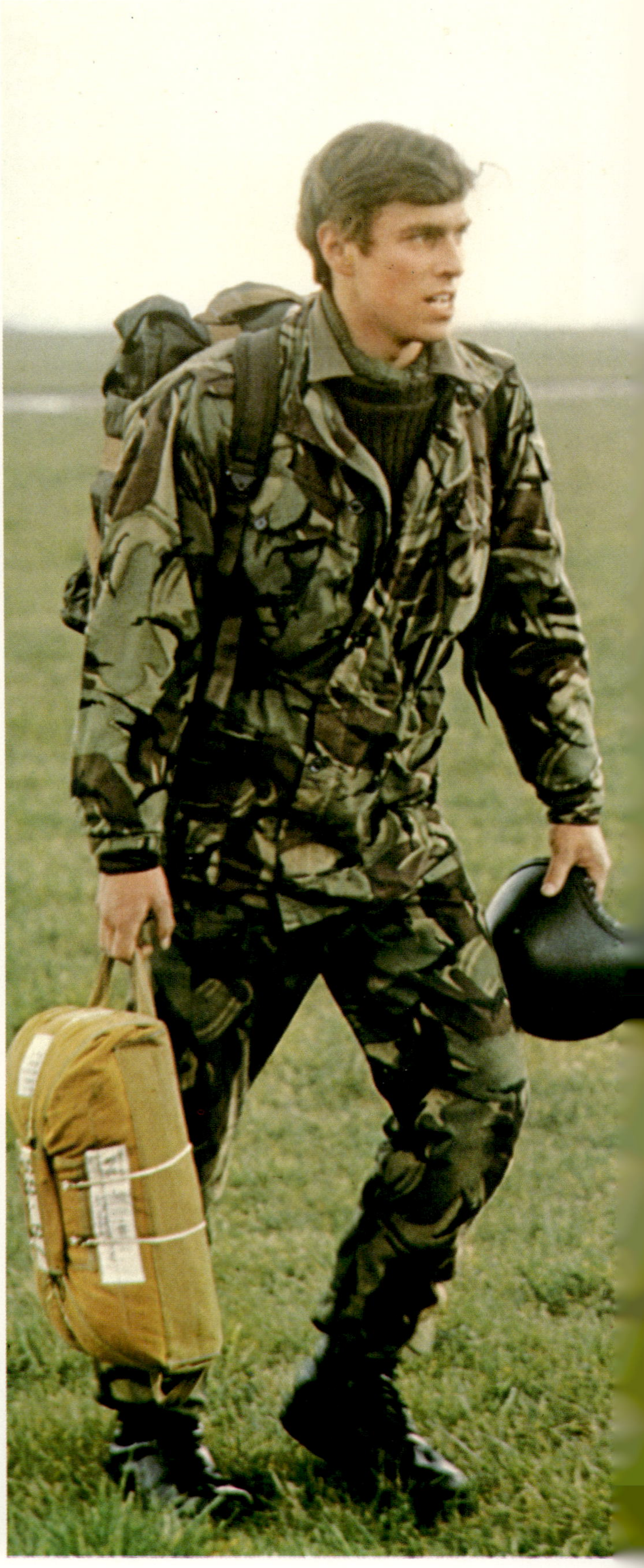

Opposite left *During the 1978 Easter holidays, Prince Andrew joined Prince Charles on a parachute training course. Here he is suspended from a mock parachute.*
Opposite right *Parachute in hand, Prince Andrew prepares to board the aeroplane from which he will make his parachute jump.*
Above *Prince Charles and Prince Andrew seen together during the parachute training course. They enjoyed a friendly rivalry, and were both awarded their Parachutist Wings.*
Right *Prince Andrew shows his Parachutist Certificate of Competence to RAF Officers. The course was taken at RAF Brize Norton, Oxfordshire.*

Private Life

Prince Andrew and Prince Edward, although close in age, are very different in character. Prince Andrew is an extrovert and revels in the company of his family and friends. In contrast, Prince Edward seems shy and gentle but, given time, will probably rival his brothers in charm. He is fond of sports, particularly ball games, and loves to fish and swim.

Free of the many restraints imposed on the heir to the throne, Prince Andrew enjoys enormous popularity, especially with the girls of his acquaintance! He also has the advantages of being both good-looking and the tallest man in the Royal family. During his time at Gordonstoun, the Prince enjoyed his studies as well as mixing with boys and girls alike, and now at nineteen he is a young, handsome man filled with a zest for life. To some, Prince Charles, at thirty-one, seems more sober, but he also has a high sense of duty and purpose spiced with a sense of humour which make him both a delightful companion for young and old.

Prince Edward is self-contained and becomes absorbed in anything he undertakes, from fly fishing, which his grandmother taught him, to photography. He is a sports enthusiast, enjoying skiing, and sailing, as well as the Royal sport of riding. The youngest member of the family knows the part he has to play and is never far behind the example set by his elder brothers.

Opposite The Queen with Prince Philip, Prince Andrew and Prince Edward in the grounds of Balmoral Castle in the summer of 1972.
Right An early photograph of Prince Andrew getting to grips with a polo stick.
Below The young Prince Andrew at a polo match with his grandmother and Princess Anne.

41

Left *During a break in his polo match, the Duke of Edinburgh talks to Prince Edward near the waiting ponies.*
Below *The Duke of Edinburgh and his youngest son, Prince Edward, deep in conversation while they watch the Badminton Horse Trials.*

Above *The Prince seen with his father at the Badminton Horse Trials.*
Right *Prince Andrew enjoying the sunshine at the Badminton Horse Trials.*

Below *A formal study of the Royal family standing in one of the splendid doorways at Buckingham Palace.*

Opposite *An informal study of the Royal family. Prince Edward takes the chair, while the Queen and Prince Andrew sit on the arms, with Prince Charles, Prince Philip and Princess Anne standing behind them all.*

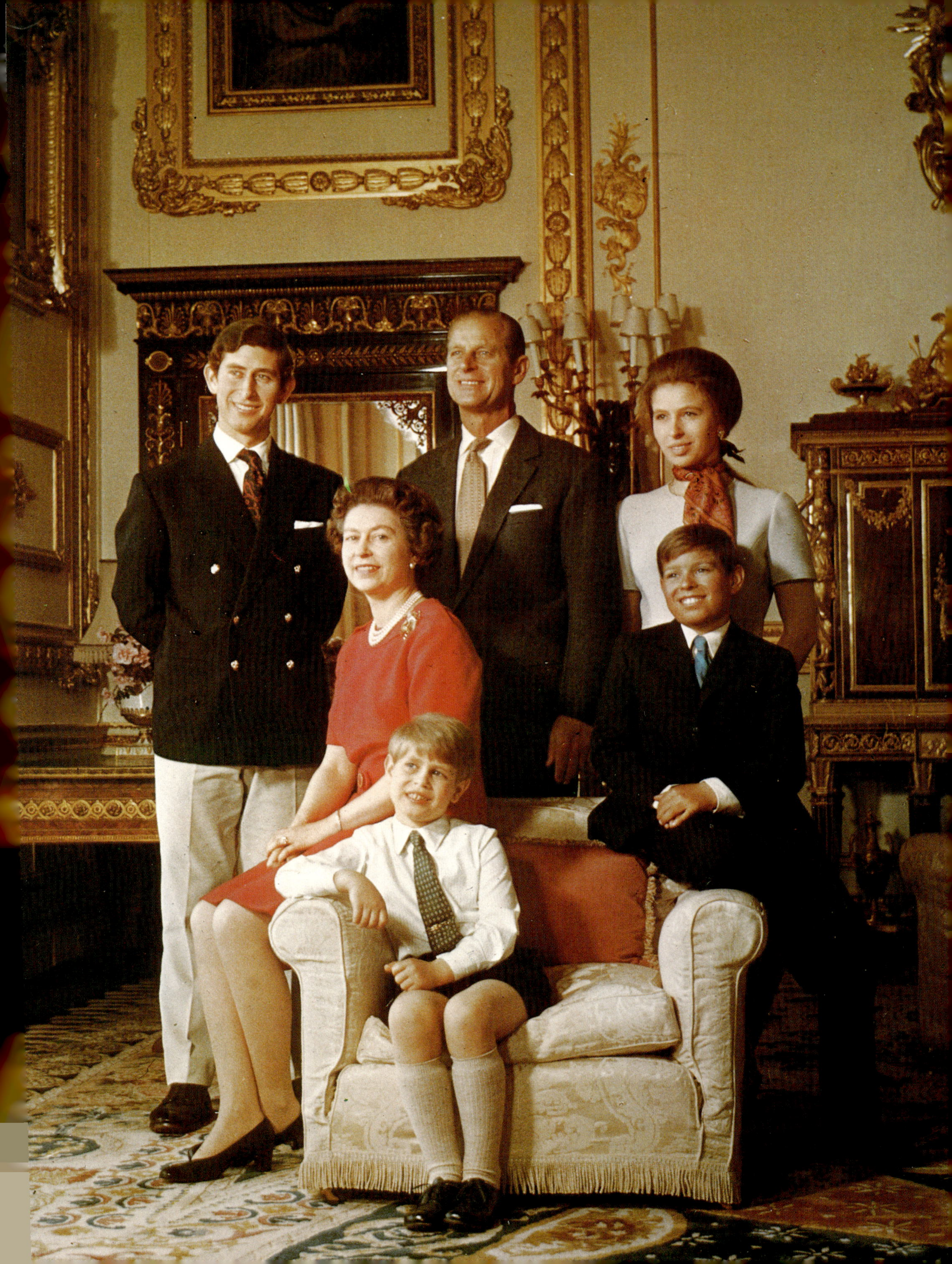

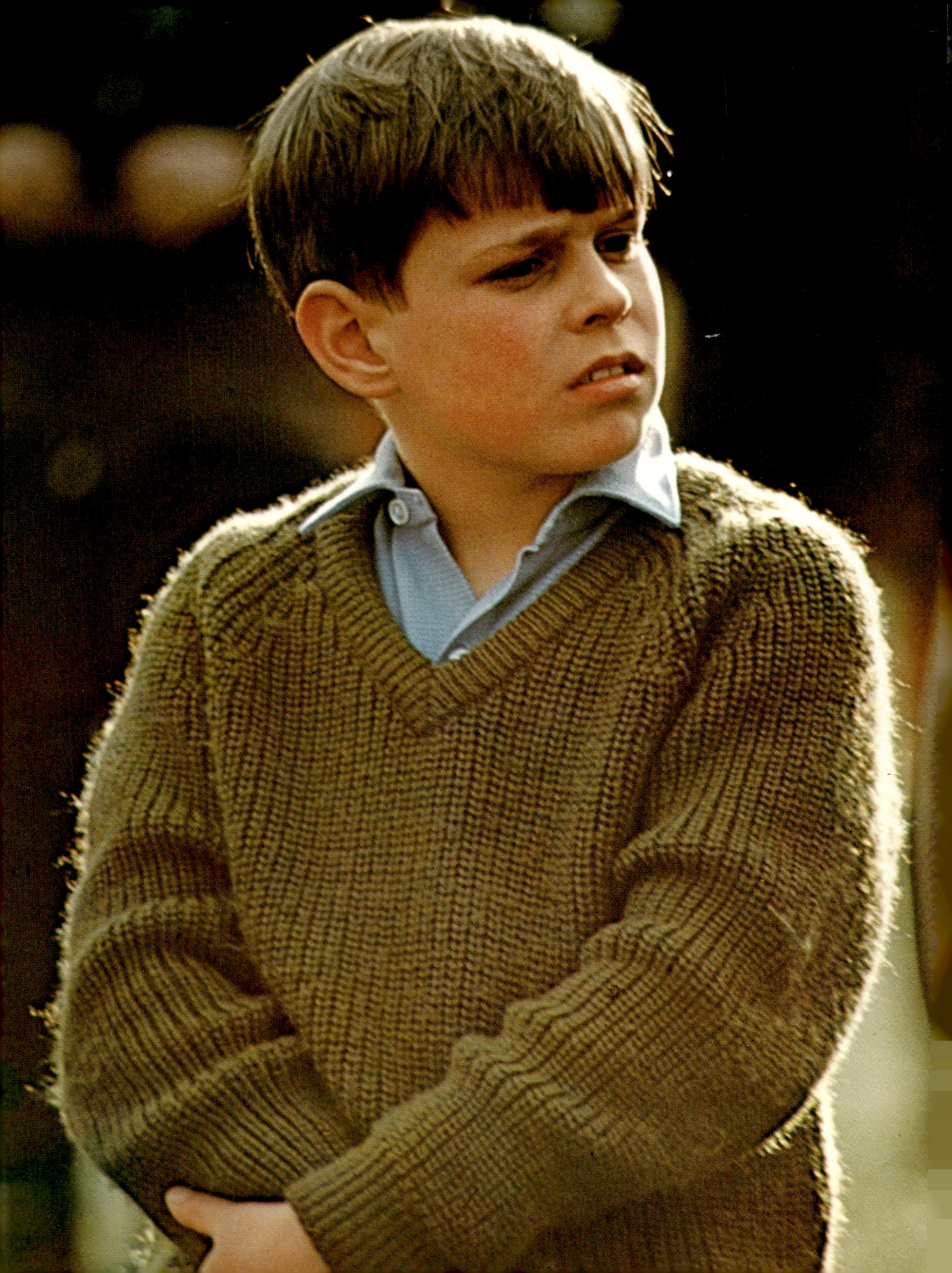

Opposite A delightful study of the young Prince Andrew in a pensive mood.
Right Prince Andrew, Prince Edward and their father, the Duke of Edinburgh, at the Badminton Horse Trials.
Below With his father by his side, Prince Edward uses field glasses to get a better view of the Badminton Horse Trials in 1977.

Above *A serious Prince Edward standing by the competitors' instruction board at the Badminton Horse Trials in 1977.*
Right *The Duke of Edinburgh, with Princess Alexandra and Prince Edward, sitting on the roof of a Range Rover to gain a better view of the Badminton Horse Trials in 1977.*
Opposite *Prince Edward applauding at the Badminton Horse Trials.*

48

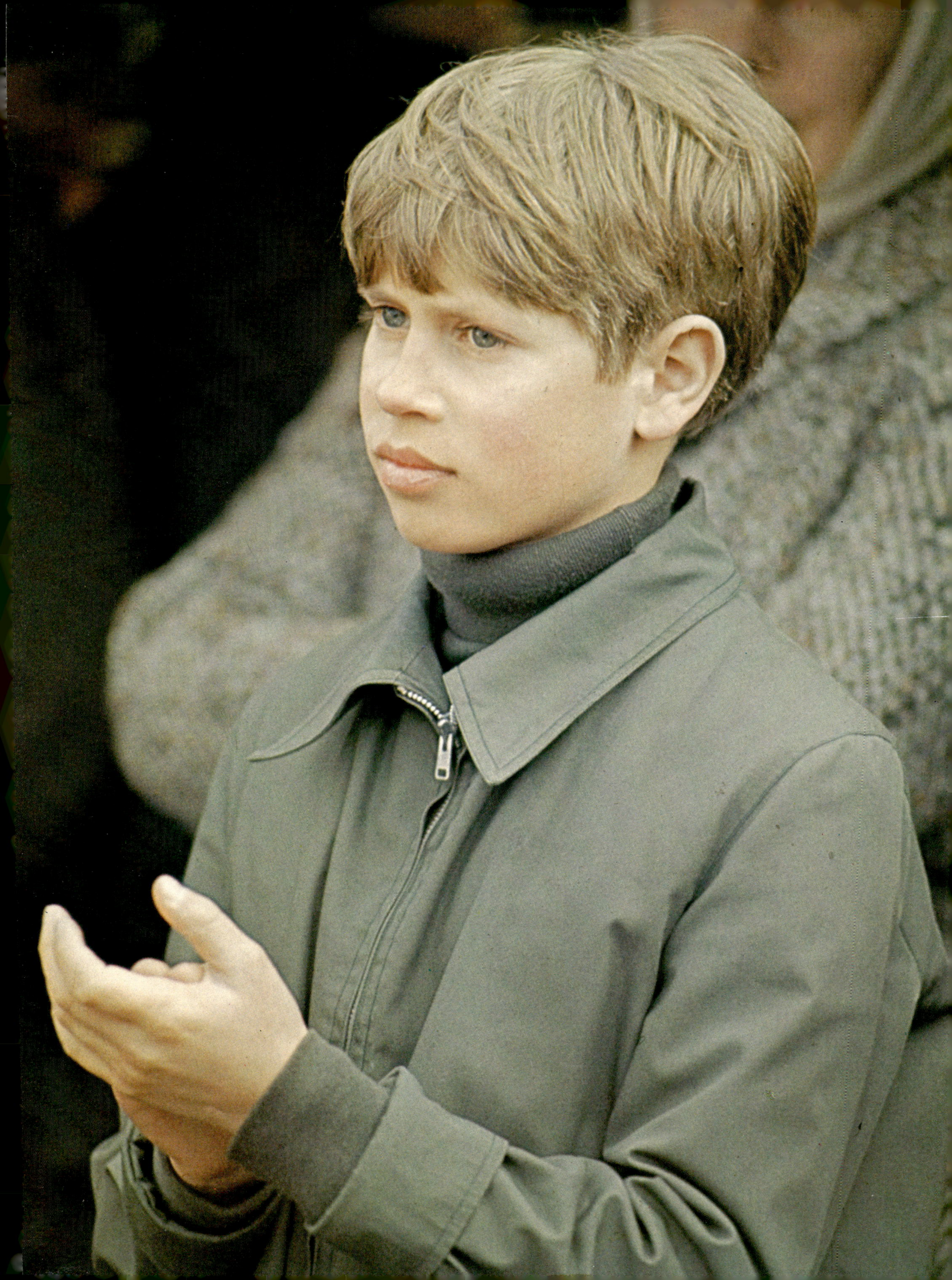

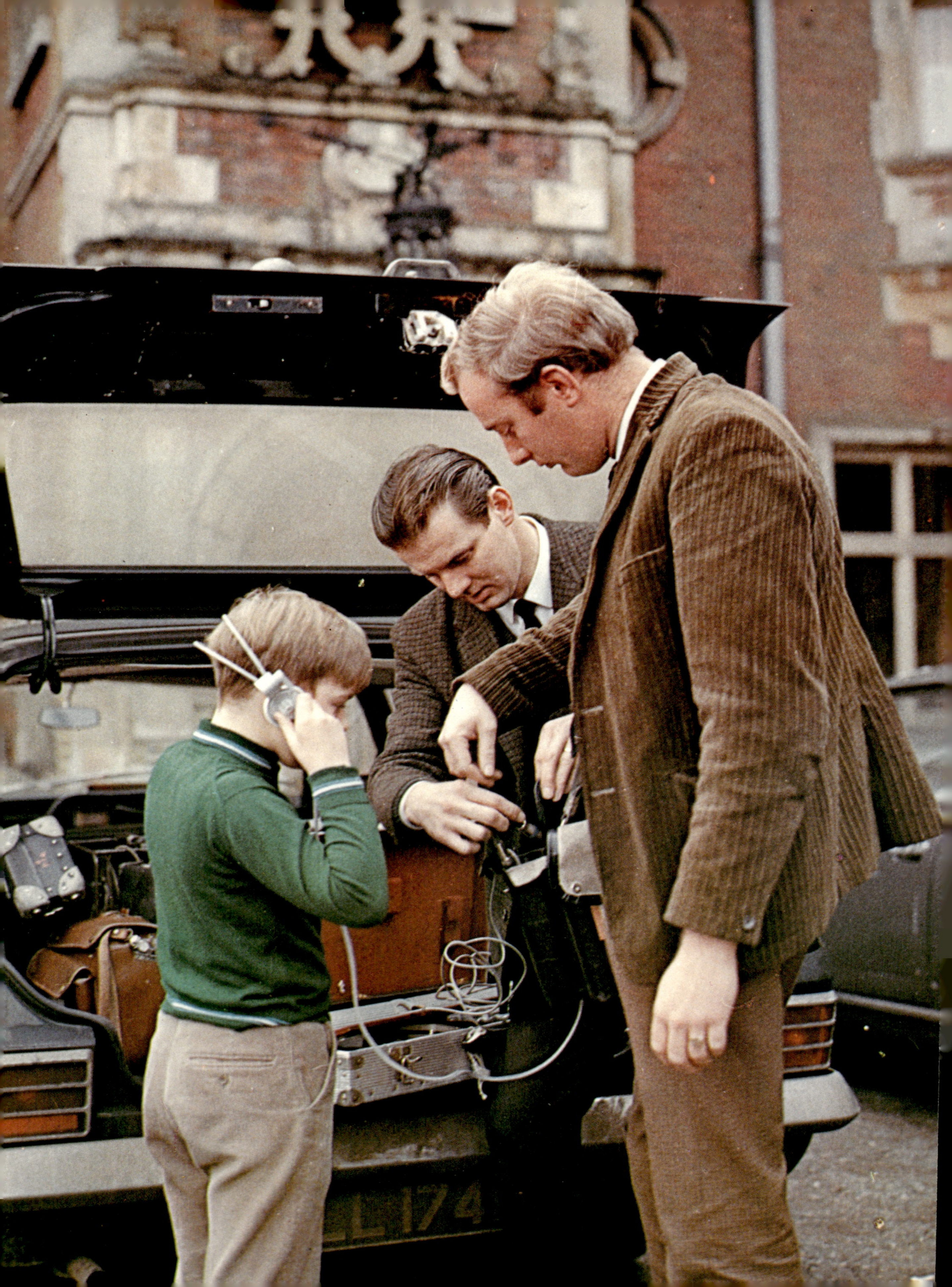

Opposite *The nine-year-old Prince Andrew with a BBC sound recordist playing back a tape during the making of the film,* Royal Family, *in 1969.* Above *Princess Anne and Prince Andrew standing together at an official function.* Right *The Duke of Edinburgh and Prince Andrew enjoying an outdoor event.*

Overleaf *Prince Edward helps his brother Prince Charles steer a go-kart round the track.*

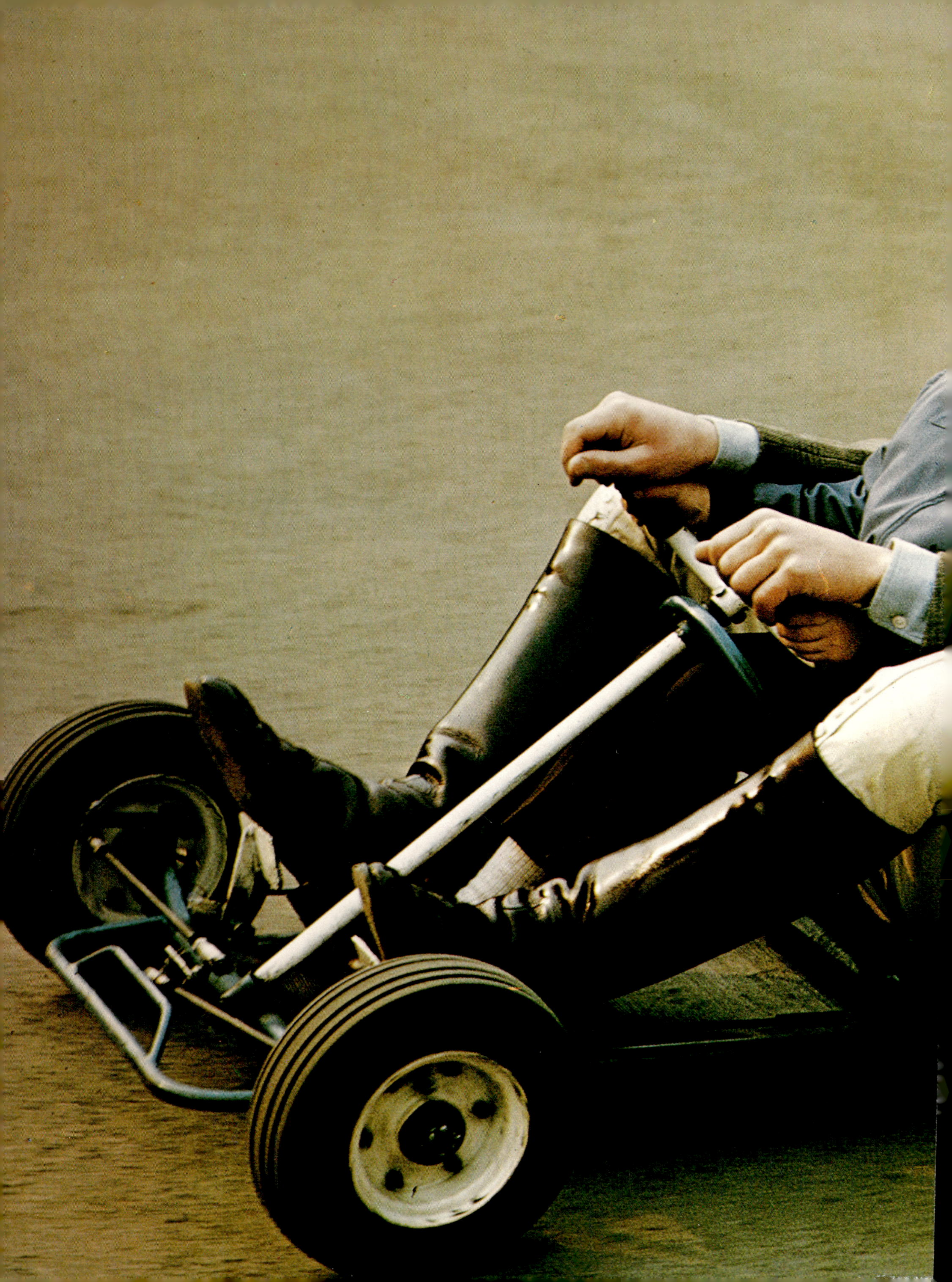

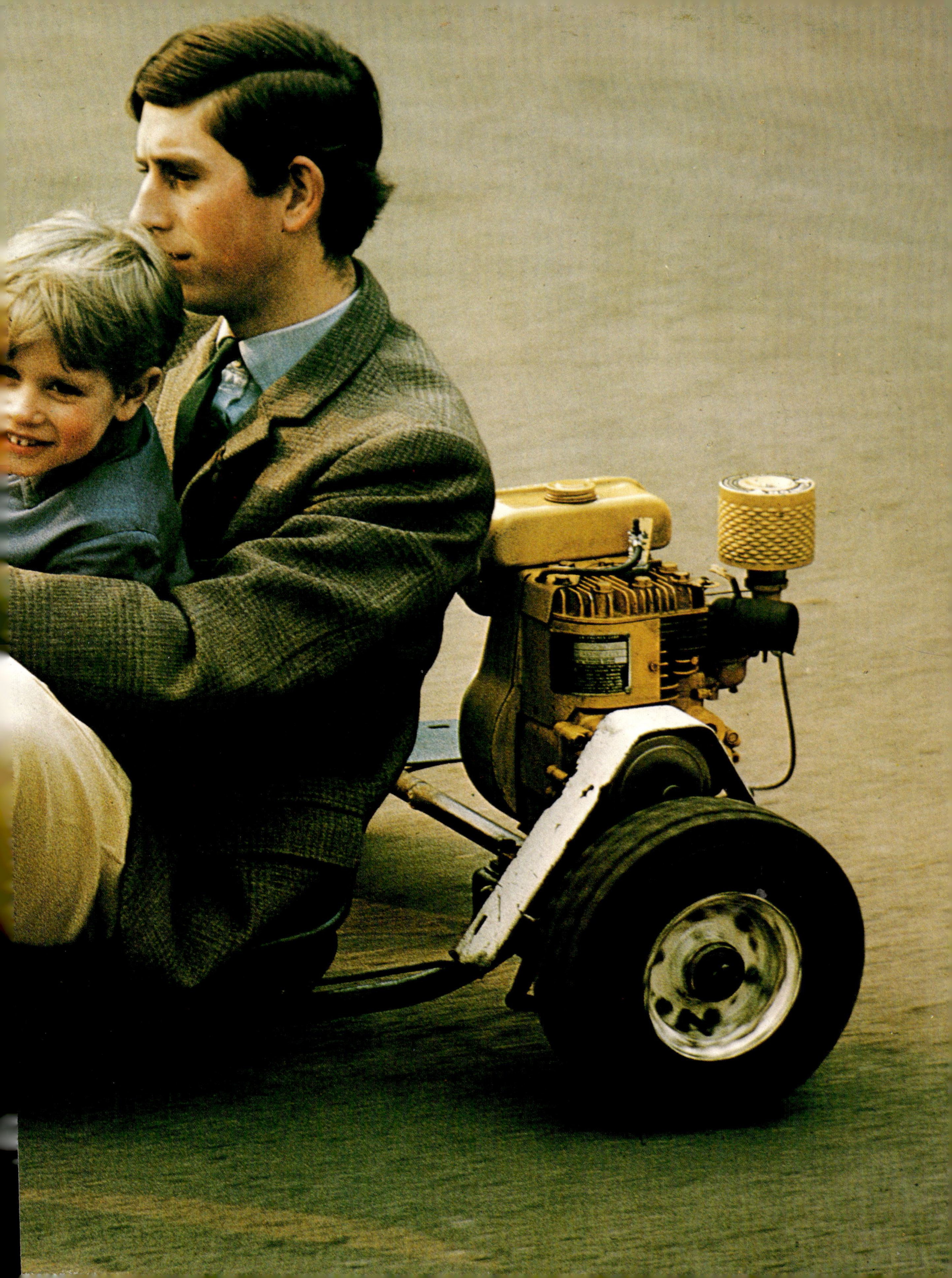

Below *An informal picture of Prince Andrew taken in Canada.*

Opposite *Prince Andrew, like his father and elder brother, is a keen sailor. Here he is helping to rig the dinghy before going sailing. He has taken part in the Cowes Regatta several times.*

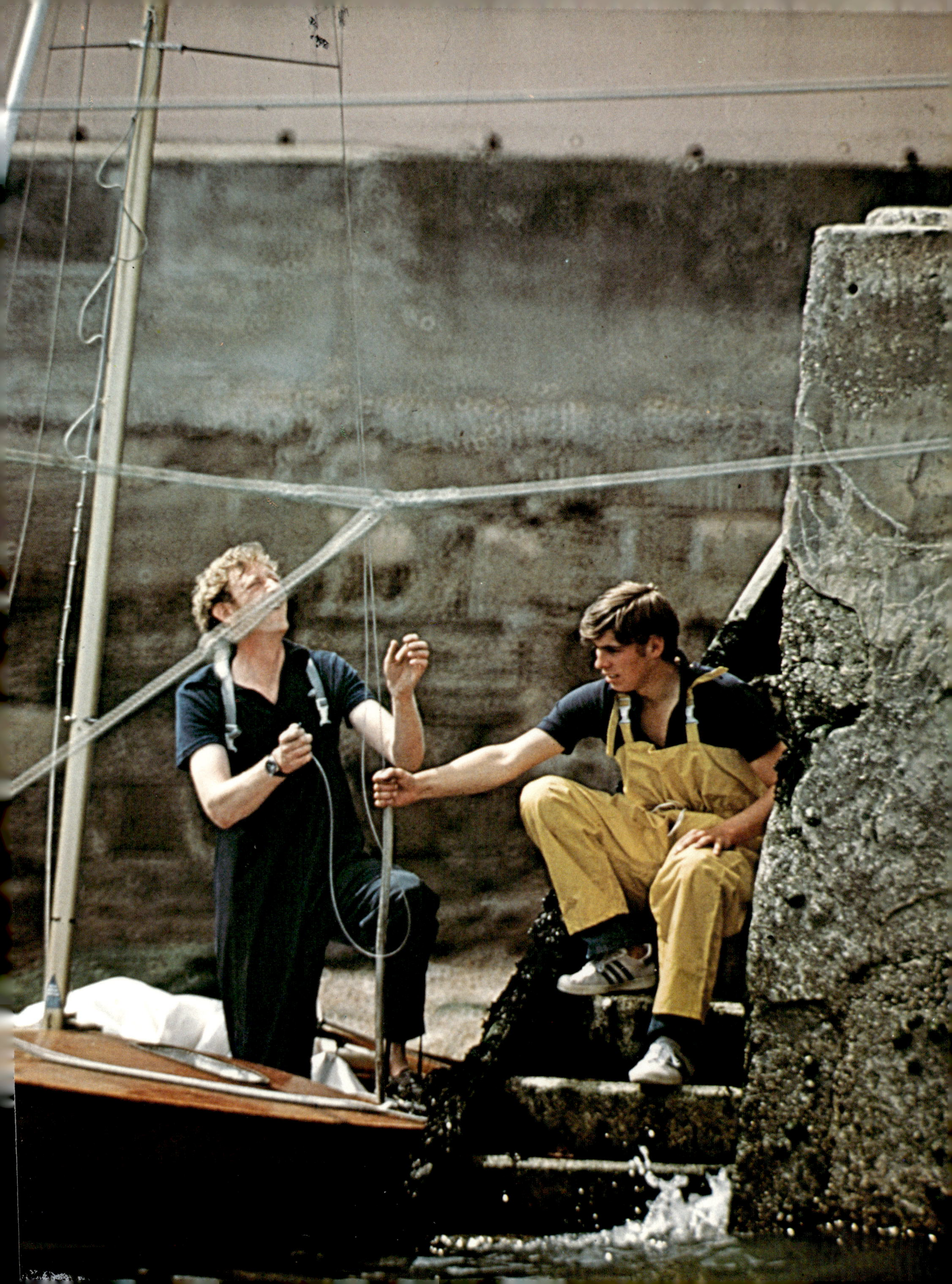

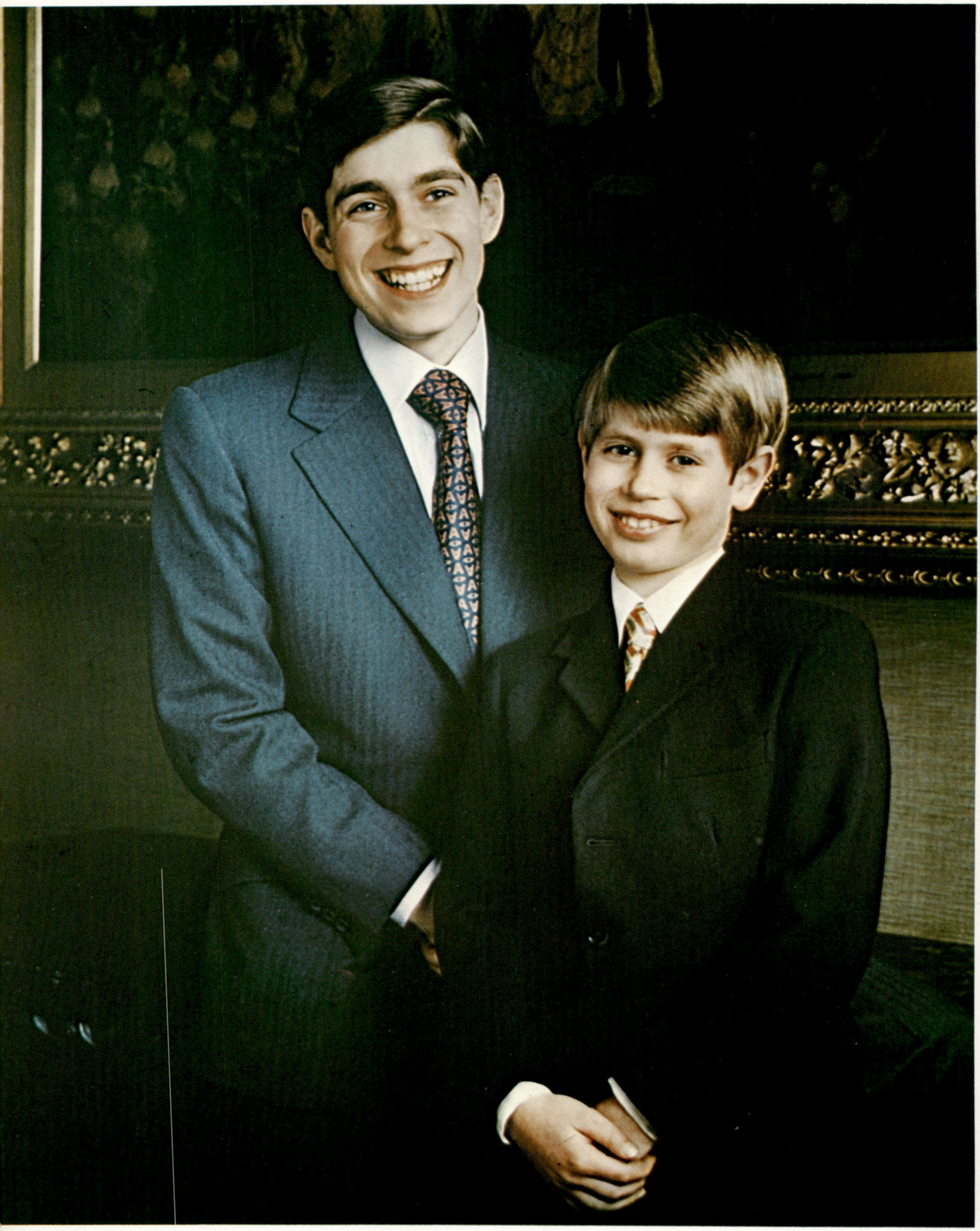

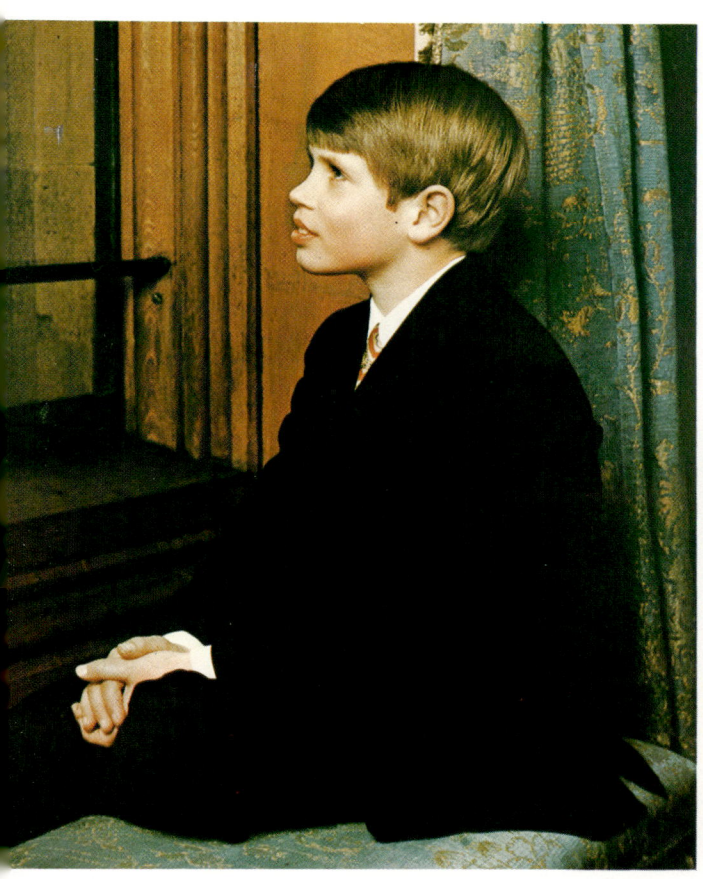

Opposite *A portrait of Prince Andrew and Prince Edward taken in 1975.*
Left *A serious study of Prince Edward taken in 1975.*
Below left *Prince Andrew in 1975.*
Below *An eighteenth birthday portrait of Prince Andrew at his desk in 1978.*

Below *A recent portrait of Prince Edward.*

Opposite *Another eighteenth birthday portrait of Prince Andrew taken in 1978.*

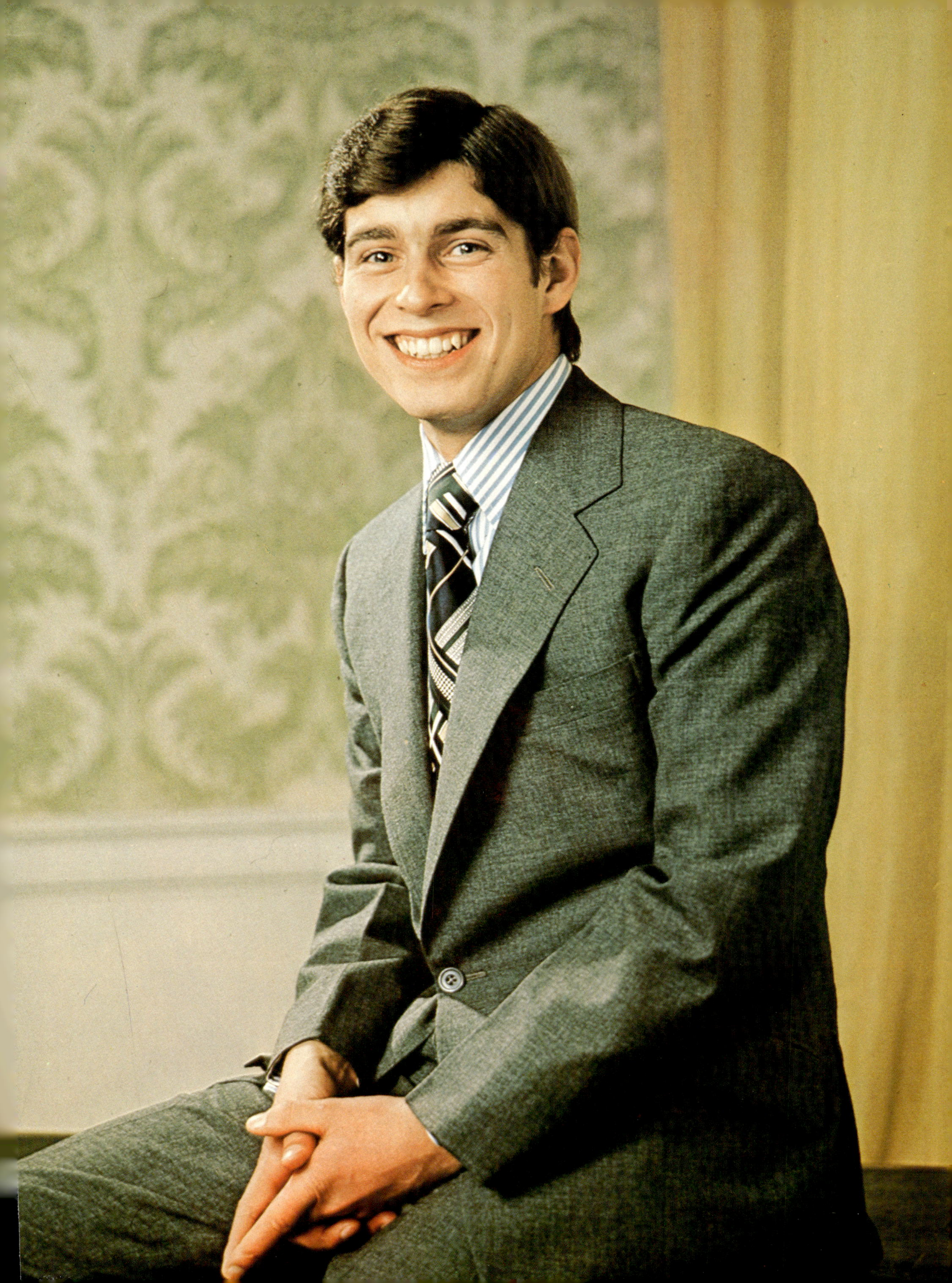

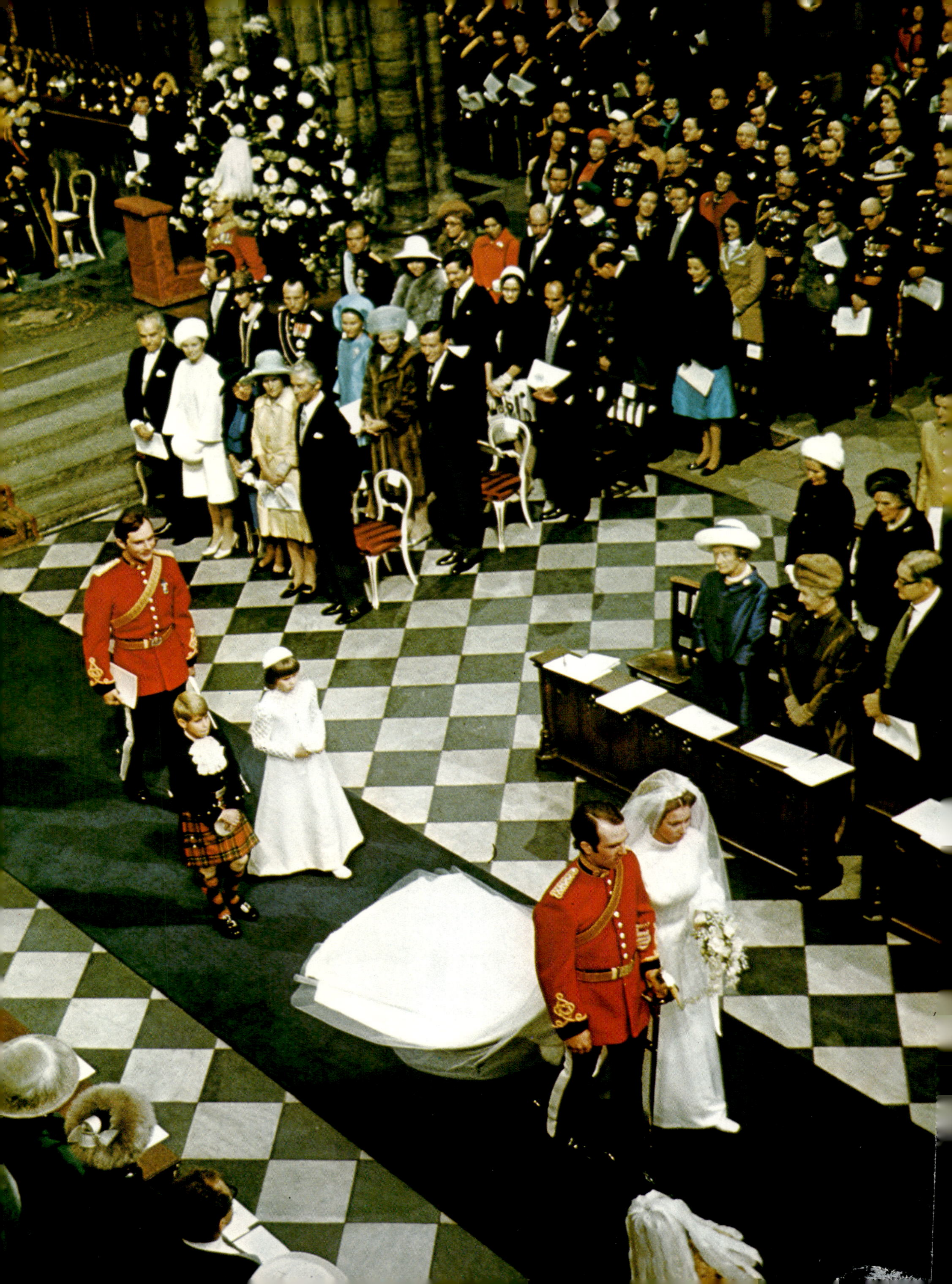

Opposite *A happy occasion at Westminster Abbey in 1973. Prince Edward was page to his sister, Princess Anne, on the occasion of her wedding to Captain Mark Phillips. The date was also the twenty-fifth birthday of Prince Charles.*

Below *Prince Andrew at the wheel of a Range Rover. He was taught to drive by the late Graham Hill.*

61

Left Prince Andrew, off on holiday to Balmoral, waves to the crowds when embarking at Southampton. He is wearing his Canadian Lakefield College sweatshirt.
Below Prince Andrew enjoying an energetic game of rugby at Lakefield College in Canada.
Opposite above The thirteen-year-old Prince Edward at the wheel of a speedboat in the Solent during Cowes Week in 1977.
Opposite below Prince Andrew seen wearing the uniform of a midshipman in the Royal Navy for the first time in public. He is with his parents, grandmother and brothers at the funeral of Lord Louis Mountbatten which took place at Westminster Abbey on 5th September 1979.

In August 1979, Prince Edward crewing for John Terry on his Flying Fifteen yacht, Crescendo, *during Cowes Week.*

Acknowledgements

The publishers would like to thank the following for their help in supplying photographs for this book.

All photographs are by courtesy of Camera Press Limited except those listed below:

Fox Photos Limited: page 12 (bottom), page 14 (bottom), page 16 (top right), pages 18–20, page 39 (bottom), page 40.

Keystone Press Agency Limited: page 25 (bottom), pages 33–34, page 38, page 39 (top), pages 52–53, page 63 (bottom).

Popperfoto: page 11 (bottom left), page 14 (top right), page 60.

The Press Association Limited: page 22 (bottom left), page 28 (bottom), page 63 (top), page 64.

Syndication International Limited: page 62 (bottom).

First English edition published 1980 by Intercontinental Book Productions, Berkshire House, Queen Street, Maidenhead, Berkshire, England
Copyright © MCMLXXX by Intercontinental Book Productions
All rights reserved
This edition is published by Crescent Books, a division of Crown Publishers, Inc, by arrangement with Intercontinental Book Productions
A B C D E F G H
Printed in Hong Kong

Library of Congress Cataloging in Publication Data

Leete-Hodge, Lornie.
   Prince Andrew and Prince Edward.

  1. Andrew, Prince of Great Britain, 1960– – Iconography. 2. Edward, Prince of Great Britain, 1964– – Iconography. 3. Great Britain – Princes and princesses – Iconography. I. Title.
DA591.A45A524   1980   941.085′092′4 [B]   79-26618
ISBN 0-517-30809-6